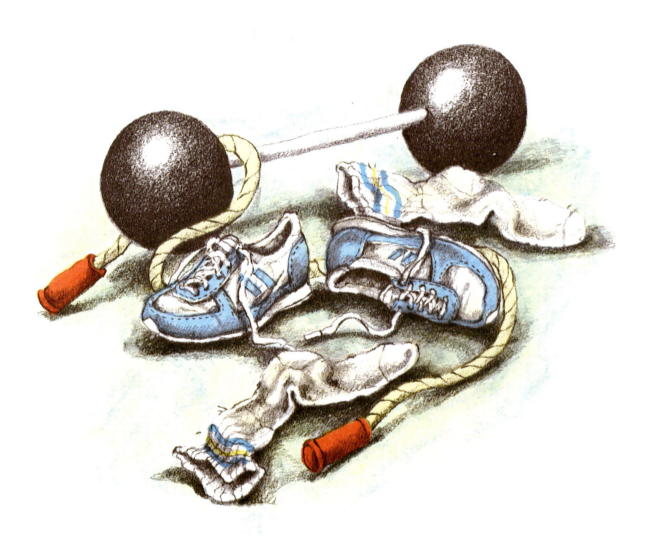

An Aesop Fable
adapted and illustrated by

Janet Stevens

SRA

Columbus, OH

The Tortoise
and the Hare

SRAonline.com

McGraw Hill SRA

Printed in Mexico.

Send all inquiries to:
SRA/McGraw-Hill
4400 Easton Commons
Columbus, OH 43219-6188

ISBN 978-0-07-612496-1
MHID 0-07-612496-7

2 3 4 5 6 7 RRM 13 12 11 10 09

Once upon a time, there was a tortoise and a hare.

Tortoise was friendly and quiet. He did everything slowly. Hare was flashy and rude. He did everything quickly.

Hare liked to tease Tortoise about being so slow.

When Tortoise ate breakfast, Hare said, "By the time you finish your last bite, it will be dinnertime."

When Tortoise worked in his garden, Hare said, "By
the time you pick those spring flowers, it will be winter."

One afternoon, Hare followed Tortoise to the store.
Hare teased him on the way. "By the time you get there, the
store will be closed," he said. "You're so slow, I could beat
you at a race, hopping backwards on one paw."

"But I could never beat you, Hare," said Tortoise.
"Yes, you could," said Tortoise's friends. "All you need is a little help."
"Then you *will* race me, Tortoise?" asked Hare.

Tortoise pulled his head into his shell.

"I don't want to," he said.

"You've got to," said his friends. "You've put up with that nasty hare long enough. We think you can win."

Tortoise didn't want to disappoint his friends, so he finally agreed to race against Hare.

Tortoise only had two-and-a-half weeks to get in shape before the big race. Rooster helped him out at the gym. Raccoon cooked him healthy meals.

Frog went jogging with him every morning.
By the day of the race, Tortoise was ready.

Animals from all over the county came to watch the tortoise and the hare.

Rooster read aloud the rules and described the course.

"Attention, everyone. The race will begin when I sound this gong. The six-mile course is marked by red flags. The first one to reach the finish line wins. Runners, take your mark, get set, GO!! Raccoon sounded the gong.

Hare bolted out of sight before Tortoise had taken his first step. The crowd roared and cheered as Tortoise inched forward.

Hare was so far ahead that he decided to stop at
Bear's house for something cool to drink.

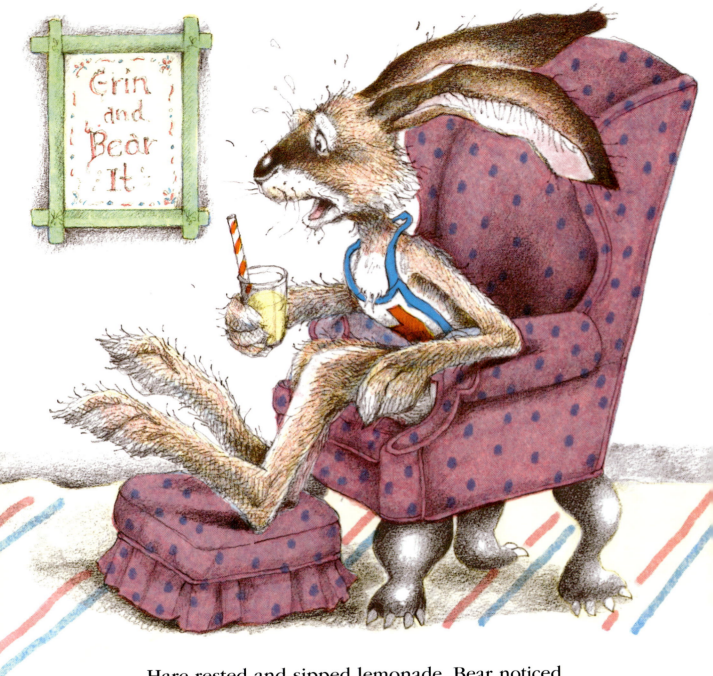

Hare rested and sipped lemonade. Bear noticed something moving outside the window. "Hare, there goes Tortoise."

"What?" yelled Hare, running out the door.

Hare passed Tortoise for the second time. Then he decided to stop at Mouse's house for a snack.

As Hare munched on crackers and cheese, Mouse yelled, "Is that Tortoise I see out the window?"

"I'm not worried about that slowpoke," said Hare. "I've passed him twice already." Then he finished his snack and hopped out the door.

Hare passed Tortoise for a third time. Now, he was far ahead. He saw a pond and decided to stop and rest. The snacks had made him sleepy.

Hare was so sure that he would win, he took a nap in the soft grass. As he closed his eyes, he dreamed of victory.

Suddenly, Hare woke up because the crowd was
cheering.

"Yay, Tortoise," the crowd roared.

Tortoise was two steps away from the finish line.

"Slow down, you bowlegged reptile," screamed Hare
as he tried to catch up.

TORTOISE

But it was too late. Tortoise crossed the line just before the tornado of dust and fur that was Hare flew by. Tortoise had won the race. Hare couldn't believe it. That measly shell on legs had beaten him.

Tortoise smiled as his friends carried him on their shoulders. He had learned an important lesson:
HARD WORK AND PERSEVERANCE BRING REWARD.